D0217837

Tudor and Stuart Gardens

Tudor and Stuart Gardens

Anne Jennings

ENGLISH HERITAGE

IN ASSOCIATION WITH THE MUSEUM OF GARDEN HISTORY

Front cover: **Vertumnus and Pomona *(1638) by David Teniers the Elder***

Back cover: **Broad-leaved everlasting pea, Lathyrus latifolius**

Published by English Heritage, 23 Savile Row, London W1S 2ET
in association with the Museum of Garden History, Lambeth Palace Road,
London SE1 7LB

Copyright © English Heritage and Museum of Garden History

Anne Jennings is hereby identified as the author of this work and asserts
her moral right to be recognised as the copyright holder in the text.

First published 2005

ISBN 1 85074 936 1
Product code 50996

A CIP catalogue for this book is available from the British Library

All rights reserved

No part of this publication may be reproduced or transmitted in any form
or by any means, electronic or mechanical, including photocopying,
recording or any information storage or retrieval system, without
permission in writing from the publisher.

Edited and brought to press by Susan Kelleher and René Rodgers
Designed by Michael McMann
Technical editor Rowan Blaik
Printed by Bath Press

CONTENTS

Introduction

This book explores the development of gardens during the Tudor and Stuart periods. It traces the gradual movement from the simple enclosed gardens of the late medieval age to the more elaborate designs of the Tudor and Stuart years. British royalty had great influence on garden design throughout the 16th and 17th centuries. Gardens created for Henry VIII reflected new ideas inspired by the Italian Renaissance and by formal French gardens. Such influences continued into the Elizabethan period, although with greater sophistication in both architectural and horticultural design. The garden increasingly became a symbol of its owner's status, sophistication and learning. When the throne passed to James I in 1603, the Stuart age began and the even more elaborate Jacobean style of architecture developed. This had enormous impact on garden-making, with new ideas developing about designing landscapes to complement great Jacobean houses. As the 17th century progressed, there was a greater emphasis on scale and simplicity, with a move toward classically inspired design in both buildings and gardens.

Practical 'how-to' sections in the book provide tips on creating Tudor- and Stuart-style features in your own garden, and the lists of plants and trees available to gardeners from this period will help to evoke an authentic feel. The availability of plants in UK nurseries is also given.

Formal planting styles like knot gardens, which were first seen in the Tudor period, are still popular today

Spectet, siue omen, non potuit melius.
Principibus nostris uberrima tempora spodet
& Phoebus radiis & Iouis uxor aquis.

The Tudor and Stuart years marked important changes in British culture and society. Following the Wars of the Roses and the defeat of the Yorkist Richard III on Bosworth Field in 1485, Henry VII succeeded to the throne. This first Tudor monarch ruled over a nation whose people were becoming increasingly better educated and cultured. Renaissance ideas from mainland Europe had already reached Britain and were being eagerly explored by the wealthy, with literature, music, art, science, architecture and ultimately gardens all influenced by these new ideas. While the country remained at relative peace with itself – if not its mainland European neighbours – there was the opportunity to indulge in these luxurious cultural pastimes and, as the 16th and 17th centuries progressed, the gentry became increasingly intellectual. An effective way of demonstrating wealth, status and knowledge was to create magnificent gardens, laid out in the latest French and Italian fashions.

Henry VIII inherited the throne on the death of his father in 1509 and the religious and political changes he introduced still influence the character and culture of Britain today. Thwarted on more than one occasion by the Catholic Church, Henry succeeded in his aim of finally separating Britain from Rome and made himself supreme head of the new Church of England. On his instruction, Thomas Cromwell implemented the Dissolution of the Monasteries, which brought about the

Manuscript illumination that combines Henry VIII's Tudor rose with the pomegranate of Catherine of Aragorn

violent destruction of all monasteries, nunneries and abbeys in the country. In addition to being places of religious activity, these had for centuries offered crucial support to surrounding communities, providing food, shelter and medicine to those in need. Their destruction also saw the end of generations of horticultural expertise, as the monks had been fine gardeners, growing herbs, fruit and flowers for medicinal, culinary and decorative use.

As the monasteries were destroyed, land that had been owned and worked by the monks was sold cheaply or gifted to local landowners and other wealthy and well-connected individuals. With land available to them, they were able to

Tantalising glimpses of a Tudor garden can be seen through the arched doorways in this painting, The Family of Henry VIII

build grand homes, alongside which magnificent gardens were made. Henry VIII himself created extravagant gardens, most notably at Hampton Court Palace and Nonsuch Palace in Surrey (which unfortunately no longer exists). These were laid out in intricate and elaborate style, inspired by grand Italian and French gardens of the early and mid-16th century, such as those at the Château de Fontainebleau.

Elizabeth I came to the throne in 1558, 11 years after the death of her father, Henry VIII, and remained queen until she died in 1603. Such a long reign provided a degree of stability and continuity within the nation and this hard-working, popular monarch strove for peace, at both national and international levels. It is evident throughout history that garden-making is at its most energetic during times of peace and, with a better educated middle and upper class eager for a more cultured way of life, it is perhaps not surprising that garden-making became a fashionable pursuit in Elizabethan England.

However, such peaceful times were not to last for many years after the death of Elizabeth I, which marked the end of the Tudor reign and the start of the Stuart line. The throne passed to Elizabeth's cousin, James I (then James VI of Scotland), the son of Mary, Queen of Scots, thus finally uniting Scotland and England. On his death in 1625, his son, Charles I, became king

A 17th-century painting by Hendrick Danckerts showing John Rose, the King's Gardener, presenting Charles II with the first pineapple grown in England

and during his reign, conflict between the king and Parliament led to the Civil War that ran from 1642–60. These were turbulent times for England, resulting in the execution of Charles I in 1649. His son, Charles II, was exiled and political upheaval continued until he was restored to the throne in 1660. The great gardens that had in earlier times been created by royalty – or with their patronage and support – were obvious targets for anti-Royalist aggression during the Civil War and enormous acts of destruction and vandalism took place. When Charles II finally became king, some form of peace returned to the country and attention could once more be lavished on ornamental gardening.

When Charles II died in 1685, his brother James II came to the throne. James II was an unpopular king, whose reign introduced the threat of a future Catholic monarch, and civil unrest resulted in his abdication following the Glorious Revolution of 1688. His daughter, Mary II, and her Dutch Protestant husband, William of Orange (William III), were invited to rule as joint monarchs, thus securing a future Protestant line. Both were interested in gardening and, under their influence, elements of Dutch garden design came to Britain.

Mary II died in 1694 and, on William's death in 1702, Mary's sister Anne came to the throne. She did not share the horticultural passion or extravagance of her predecessors and, in fact, cut spending on royal gardens dramatically. When she died in 1714 the first German king, George I, came to the throne and thus began the Georgian period, when a completely different style of horticulture developed in Britain.

Thus the Tudor and Stuart periods were not only marked by great political and social change, but they were also a time when ornamental gardening began to excite the enthusiasm of British people, from the top levels of society, filtering down to what would later be termed the middle classes. Combined with an obsession for stylish gardens, a fascination for 'new' plants developed, and these two key components were to create a strong character to gardens of the 16th and 17th centuries that is still admired and copied today.

FLORILEGIVM

Ab Hadriano Collaert cælatum, et à Philip. Galleo editum.

ILLVSTRISS. ECCELENTISSIMOQVE DÑO D. IOANNI MEDICI. OMNIS GENERIS ELEGANTIARVM AD: MIRATORI ET PATRONO, PHILIP. GALLÆVS DD.

Tudor and Stuart writers on gardens

Contemporary books, pamphlets and leaflets, often embellished with intricate illustrations cut from wood blocks, provide an important source of information on Tudor and Stuart life, including details about plants and gardens of the period. Paper was readily available by the mid-15th century and, with the development of early printing presses, books were becoming increasingly available to the general public.

Thomas Hill (c 1529–75) was one of the first writers to produce popular gardening books that provided detailed information on horticultural design and practice. His first book, published in 1563, bore the cumbersome title *A most brief and pleasaunte Treatyse, teachynge howe to Dress, Sowe, and set a Garden*, but it was later republished as *The Proffitable Arte of Gardening*. The original version includes the first bird's eye view of a garden seen in an English gardening book and gives a clear idea of what a Tudor garden looked like, with a knot design surrounded by flower beds and enclosed by ornate trellis.

Hill's *The Gardener's Labyrinth* was published in 1577 and remained popular for many years, with the last edition printed in 1660. It was a practical manual with chapters dedicated to choosing a site, digging, levelling and manuring beds, seed sowing, watering, weeding and pest control, as well as

'The air and genius of gardens operate upon the human spirit towards virtue and sanctity.'

Title page of Florilegium *(1590), a book of floral drawings compiled by Adrian Collaert and Philip Galleo*

Place this knot in fol. 189.

A propze knot foz a Garden, where as is fpare rowme enough, the whiche may be fet either with Tyme, oz Ifope, at the difcre= tion of the Gardener.

instructing on the layout and design of knots and other garden features.

'A propre knot for a Garden' from Thomas Hill's The Proffitable Arte of Gardening

> *The gardener minding to trie and know a fat*
> *earth, for the use of a Garden, shall worke after*
> *this manner: in taking a little clod of the earth,*

and the same to sprinkle with fair water,
kneading it well in the hand: which after
appearing clammie, and cleaving or sticking to
the fingers, doth undoubtedly witnesse the earth
to have a fatness in it.

The Gardener's Labyrinth, Thomas Hill, 1577

Francis Bacon (1561–1626) was a writer, lawyer and politician, with a love of science and an interest in gardens. He wrote an essay in 1625 entitled *Of Gardens*, which detailed his vision of what a garden should be, although his description to some extent contradicted the reality of Jacobean gardens of the time. Knot gardens were still very fashionable when Bacon was writing, but he states 'they be but toys; you may see as good sights many times in tarts'. He criticises the use of topiary when cut into figures but finds 'pretty pyramids' and 'fair column' acceptable.

God Almighty first planted a garden; and indeed
it is the purest of human pleasures. It is the
greatest refreshment of the spirits of man,
without which buildings and palaces are but
gross handiworks.

Of Gardens, Francis Bacon, 1625

Externall wilfull evils are these.

1 Walls.

2 Trenches.

3 Other works noisome done in or neere

4 Evill Neighbours.   (your Orchard.

5 A carelesse Master.

6 An undiscreet, negligent or no keeper.

See you here an whole army of mischiefes banded in troupes against the most fruitfull trees the earth beares, assailing your good labours.   Good things have most enemies.

Illustration from the 1638 edition of William Lawson's A New Orchard or Garden, *first published in 1618, showing the planting of an orchard. The text lists the 'externall wilfull evils' that could plague one's orchard.*

17th-century portrait of John Evelyn by Robert Walker

The writings of the diarist John Evelyn (1620–1706) provide valuable sources of information, not only about social history but also about Stuart gardens. He was a keen horticulturalist and made a garden at his home, Sayes Court in Deptford, Kent, that demonstrated his love and knowledge of Italian Renaissance and formal French gardens. He also made gardens at the family home, Wotton House in Surrey. He travelled to France and Italy in the mid-17th century and his diary records information about the gardens he visited, many of which inspired the design of 17th-century English gardens. Evelyn's *Sylva, or a Discourse of Forest-trees* was published in 1644, at a time when enormous tree planting was taking place in Britain, partly because of the need to replace timber stocks after severe depletion during several wars and to meet the needs of Stuart landscape designers who favoured the planting of long axial avenues of trees. Evelyn's garden encyclopaedia *Elysium Britannicum* was never published in his lifetime, although a version is available today.

Pen sketches of garden tools from John Evelyn's Elysium Britannicum

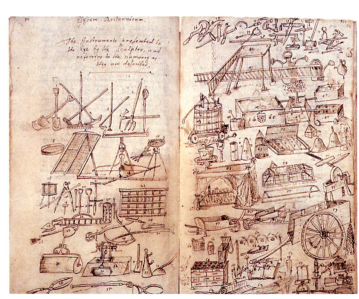

The air and genius of gardens operate upon the
human spirit towards virtue and sanctity.

John Evelyn

[A garden is a] place of all terrestriall
enjoyments the most resembling Heaven, and
the best representation of our lost felicitie…

John Evelyn

Other forms of writing from the 16th and 17th centuries tell us a great deal about Tudor and Stuart gardens. William Shakespeare (1564–1616) made many references to plants and gardens in his works, a fact that emphasises how contemporary poetry and prose can also help us understand more about gardens of any period.

Be kind and courteous to this gentleman.
Hop in his walks and gambol in his eyes;
Feed him with apricocks and dewberries,
With purple grapes, green figs,and mulberries.

Titania in *A Midsummer Night's Dream*, William Shakespeare, *c* 1595

The Italian Renaissance and garden design

The Italian Renaissance defined the culture of Italy between the 15th and 17th centuries. It was characterised by a renewed appreciation of the art, architecture and literature of ancient Greece and Rome, combined with a fascination for learning and discovery. In addition, the Renaissance embodied the beliefs of humanism, an important aspect of which was the respect of an individual irrespective of his religious beliefs. The latter was a radical philosophy in a country so dominated by the Church. This complex combination of ideas created sophisticated and influential societies, especially in the cities of Florence, Milan and Venice. Churchmen, traders, noblemen and national representatives were travelling throughout mainland Europe and Renaissance ideas and philosophies reached Britain as early as the 15th century.

The Renaissance also inspired Italian garden design and it was only a matter of time before its influence was seen in the English landscape. One of the most significant elements was the innovative idea of relating the garden to the house and vice versa. Renaissance gardens were designed specifically to enhance and complement the architecture of the house. Formal lines and simple geometric shapes dominated and structure was provided, not only by 'hard' features such as paths, walls, pools and statues, but also by 'soft' architecture, such as the hedges and topiary that were also found in

This covered walkway is part of the Privy Gardens at Hampton Court Palace, which have been restored to the original 1702 layout. This feature demonstrates how early Renaissance influence continued in later gardens (see image on p 22).

Tudor gardens in Britain. It was in this period too that 'ground patterns' created by low hedges were used in the form of knot gardens, 'foot mazes' and labyrinths; these features were also adopted and adapted with enormous enthusiasm in Britain and, apart from a period of neglect in the 18th century, have continued to be used in garden design up to the present day.

Detail of a 16th-century fresco depicting the Villa Medici and its gardens

One valuable source of information on Renaissance gardens is the writing of the Italian architect, philosopher and Latin scholar, Leon Battista Alberti (1404–72). Like many Renaissance scholars, his work drew on classical sources, including the writings of the Roman architect Marcus Vitruvius Pollio (1st century BC). Alberti based some of his ideas about architecture and gardens on Vitruvius's *Ten Books on Architecture (De Architectura)*, which was written c 27 BC. Although most of Vitruvius's references to gardens discussed the relationship between the house and surrounding land rather than detailing the specific designs for gardens, general recommendations were made. Symmetry and geometry were

View of the two villas and garden designed for Cardinal Giovanni Francesco Gambara in the 16th century, Bagnaia, Italy

highly favoured, as was the use of topiary and evergreen plants; features such as pools, sculpture and arbours were also discussed. These were all elements that could be found in Renaissance garden design.

The letters of Pliny the Younger (c AD 61–112) provided direct inspiration for Renaissance gardens. He recorded in great detail the layout and planting of the gardens surrounding his villas, one in Tuscany and the other just outside Rome. Descriptions of the views from his house emphasise the importance of the relationship between house, garden and the surrounding landscape, which was to become one of the revolutionary aspects of Italian Renaissance gardens and, in time, Tudor gardens in Britain.

> *From a corner of the portico you enter a very large bed-chamber opposite the large dining room, which from some of its windows has a view of the terrace, and from others, of the meadow, as those in front look upon a cascade, which entertains at once both the eye and the ear; for the water, dashing from a great height, foams over the marble basin which receives it below.*

Letter *LII* from Pliny the Younger to Domitius Apollinaris

Renaissance garden design also drew on Pliny's letters for information about features within the garden. In one, Pliny talks of marble fountains, rills, stone seats, arbours and columns, and such features became important elements of the Italian Renaissance garden. Similarly the letters reveal information about plants and their ornamental uses, demonstrating the importance of evergreen plants, hedges and topiary in providing structure in gardens that in general gave little prominence to flowers.

Topiary designs from the 15th-century *Hypnerotomachia Poliphili*

Another influential Renaissance book – written anonymously in 1462 and published in 1499 – was the *Hypnerotomachia Poliphili*, which is translated to mean 'The Strife of Love in a Dream'. This book records Poliphilo's dream in which he searches for his lover. The landscape he moves through is described both in text and illustrations that include lists of plants and images of knot gardens and elaborate topiary. The book was finally translated into English in 1592.

Inspired by all these ideas, Italian architects like Donato Bramante (1444–1514) incorporated the design of gardens into their building work, most notably in Bramante's case at the Vatican where he linked the Palace with Pope Julius II's Villa Belvedere. These dramatic gardens, which no longer exist, were laid out in a simple geometric manner, with central paths, cross axes and focal points and contained sculpture on

A garden scene from the Hypnerotomachia Poliphili, *with a covered trellis similar to the one seen at Hampton Court on p 16*

a grand scale, along with flights of steps, turf knots, water features and walkways.

As the 16th century progressed, Italian gardens became ever more elaborate and architects introduced drama and theatre into their designs. At the hillside Villa d'Este in Tivoli, water was used in abundance to create movement, sound and surprise. Formal pools, rows of water jets – as in the Path of One Hundred Fountains – and elaborate statuary inspired by

Roman and Greek mythology and literature added dramatic effects. In these later Renaissance gardens the designs also often integrated allegorical stories, in this case highlighting the ancient ancestry of the owners.

Detail of grotesque faces and waterway from the Path of One Hundred Fountains at the Villa d'Este

Tudor gardens

Renaissance ideas had a profound effect on English gardens, with sophisticated Tudors embracing these modern thoughts with enthusiasm. Increased wealth provided the means to invest in building houses, commissioning and buying art, and making gardens, incorporating the new styles and ideas from Italy. Renaissance-inspired garden designs began to spread north though Europe during this period, with France in particular embracing these developments.

The first move in Britain toward making homes with gardens was seen in the early 16th century, when peace in the nation meant that the fortified buildings of the Norman period were no longer needed. Instead of stone castles, royal and baronial manors were built. Although most of these remained protected to some extent, they were designed as beautiful homes surrounded by gardens. Thornbury Castle near Bristol, now a hotel, was one of the most significant transitional buildings and gardens in Britain, and owner Edward Stafford, 3rd Duke of Buckingham, created two enclosed gardens and an orchard here. There is little detailed information available about what the gardens looked like, but it is thought they were laid out in a quartered design, in the style of medieval gardens, but that features like knots and a fountain evidenced early Renaissance influence.

Rosa mundi, Rosa gallica *'Versicolor'*

Reconstructed knot garden from the Tudor House Museum and Garden in Southampton

There is not a great deal of written or illustrative evidence of what early Tudor gardens looked like and therefore certain assumptions are made about the transference of ideas and designs from mainland Europe. Henry VII's close relationship with the French courts provided a natural conduit for Renaissance ideas about gardens and it is likely that Henry's work at Richmond Palace was influenced by French palaces and gardens. The gardens at Richmond were described as:

> ...most fair and pleasant gardens, with royal knots alleyed and herbed; many marvellous beasts, as lions, dragons, and others of such divers kind, properly fashioned and carved in the ground, right well sanded, and compassed in with lead; with many vines, seeds, and strange fruit, right goodly beset, kept and nourished with much labour and diligence.

Quoted in *Medieval Gardens*, John Harvey, 1981

However, it was when Henry VIII came to the throne in 1509 that true Renaissance influence began to be seen in England and even then it took another 20 years or so before the style was adopted in all its richness and extravagance. Once Henry's reign began it quickly became apparent that he would practice excess in all he undertook, from marriage to garden-making. He was an enormously influential king whose preferences were eagerly adopted by his supporters in their anxiety to remain in favour. It is likely that the landed aristocracy throughout the country would have reproduced the style of art, architecture and gardens commissioned by the monarch himself.

Henry's love of pageantry, tournaments and fêtes highlights a focus on a social life outside the palace and it therefore seems natural that he would turn his attention to garden-making on a grand scale. He was perhaps inspired by the fashionable gardens at Thornbury Castle, and he was soon to make his mark on those started by Cardinal Thomas Wolsey at the new Hampton Court on the River Thames. As well as making improvements to the building, Henry set about developing the gardens of the palace into the finest in England.

Heraldic beasts from the Tudor House Museum and Garden in Southampton

Detail of a heraldic stag

The New Garden, or Privy Garden, situated beneath the royal apartments was enclosed by a wall and laid out in a simple geometric design with square beds divided into quarters, surrounded by walks or paths. A series of sundials reflected the fashion for introducing scientific reference into the garden and simple knot patterns were embellished, not with plants, but with coloured stones, gravel, sand and dust.

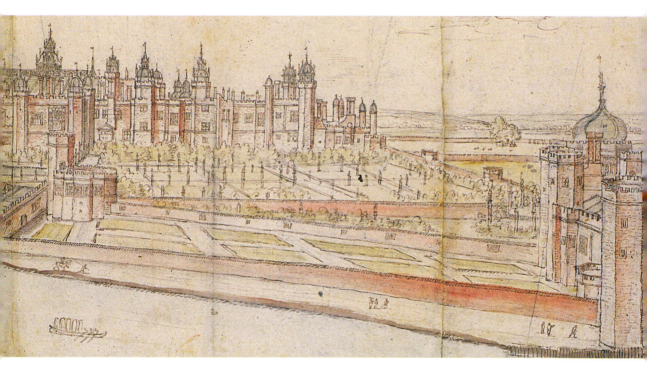

An English Tudor device, distinct from any Italian Renaissance influence, was the use of brightly painted heraldic features repeated regularly throughout the garden. Where the Italians and French used stoneware and statuary, the English monarch favoured timber posts, with the tops carved as beasts like lions, horses and dragons, and each brightly coloured and topped with a small flag that often depicted the Tudor rose. Between each post ran wooden rails, painted in the Tudor colours of green and white.

Detail from a 16th-century drawing of Hampton Court by Anthonis van Wyngaerde, which shows the New Garden laid out with heraldic beasts

Another important feature at Hampton Court was the Mount. Built in 1533, it was a development of the mounds built within the walls of medieval castles. These were originally introduced as security measures, providing views of the wider landscape from where any potential attack would come. However, in the Tudor garden, mounts became ornamental devices that formed focal features and provided elevated views of the garden from where the intricacy of the knots could be appreciated. The Mount at Hampton Court was densely planted with hawthorn through which a winding path led to the top where an arbour, three floors high, provided a protected environment. Here the king and queen could enjoy views of the Privy Garden and the Thames.

Henry VIII continued his horticultural activities at Whitehall in Westminster. This site has not survived, but fortunately some Elizabethan visitors described the gardens and what they had seen there:

> In the middle of the garden is a nice fountain with a remarkable sundial, showing the time in thirty different ways. Between the spices that are planted in the garden there are fine walks grown in grass, and the spices are planted very artistically, surrounded by plants in the shape of seats.

create Tudor heraldic timber features

The instructions below show how to create posts and rails around formal beds.

❖ Use planed timber posts approximately 4in (100mm) square for each end or corner of the bed. After treating them with preservative, apply two coats of exterior primer to the wood.

❖ The posts will look more pleasing if they are sunk directly into a hole approximately 18in (460mm) deep, filled with concrete that is neatly finished at the top. However, there is a greater risk of wood rot with this method; you could reduce this risk by inserting metal or concrete spurs into the ground and fixing the wooden posts to these.

King Henry VIII's Hampton Court garden had brightly coloured timber rails and posts that enclosed sections of the garden. To create a similar effect in your garden, use planed timber with a smooth surface, which is more suitable for paint than the rough finish of garden timber. This means you must treat all the wood you buy with a proprietary timber treatment, especially if it is to be used as posts set in the ground. Be sure to follow all the health and safety instructions on the containers or packaging of such timber treatments.

❖ The rail between the posts should be round dowel, approximately 3in (80mm) in diameter. It will also need to be treated with preservative followed by two coats of exterior primer.

❖ If you are skilled at carpentry, the rails could be fixed to the posts using joints or dowels, but if you are less experienced, simply use screws. The rails must be cut so they fit exactly between the uprights, then they can be screwed from the back of the post through to

the rail using 3in (80mm) countersunk screws. Fill the hole over the screws with exterior grade wood filler.

❖ Now for the fun bit! Using an exterior gloss or satin finish, oil-based paint, choose your background colour. This would have traditionally been white but choose any colour scheme you like. The posts and rails should be painted with two coats of this background colour.

❖ When this is completely dry, use masking tape to mark out a design using diagonal, spiral or straight lines. Select your complementary colour and paint between the masking tape guides.

❖ When this second colour is thoroughly dry, carefully remove the masking tape to reveal your completed Tudor inspired post-and-rail feature.

From 1538 to 1547 Henry focussed attention on building the new Nonsuch Palace in Surrey, the jewel in the crown of his royal residences and designed to outshine François I's Château de Fontainebleau. Few records remain of Henry's garden, but the fact that an Italian architect and French gardeners worked on the project suggests a strong European and Renaissance influence. There are references to knot gardens, arbours and 'delicate orchards', topiary beasts and a labyrinth. Inventories detail marble fountains and antique statuary, which perhaps to some extent replaced the timber features seen at Hampton Court and introduced a stronger Renaissance character to the gardens. The palace was not finished during Henry's life and eventually passed to Lord John Lumley who updated the gardens to suit later Elizabethan fashions. Both palace and garden were demolished in the late 17th century.

Both yellow and orange flowering forms of day lily were grown in Britain from c 1570

Elizabethan gardens

Gardening continued to be influenced by Renaissance fashions during Elizabeth I's reign. England had taken to ornamental gardening with enthusiasm and perhaps one of the greatest differences between early Tudor and Elizabethan gardens was the focus on plants, encouraged by the growing numbers of new species arriving from abroad. By this time merchant ships were bringing silk, cotton, exotic fruits, potatoes, tobacco, oils and spices, as well as plants and seeds to Britain.

Wealthy Elizabethans built houses on an enormous scale, with elaborate detail in the stonework, bricks, timber and plaster, and the gardens were as decorative and elaborate as the houses they enhanced. Those cared for by John Gerard at Lord Burleigh's Theobalds in Hertfordshire were said to be among the finest of the time, with a number of intimate, enclosed gardens and a large 7-acre Great Garden. This was

Venus, the goddess of love and gardens, was the inspiration for formal water features at Theobalds and at Bolsover Castle where this original 17th-century statue has been restored to its former Renaissance glory

laid out with elaborate box and grass knots surrounded by privet and hawthorn hedges. Stoneware and water features, including ornamental moats or canals, added to the formality of the garden and this use of water suggests strong Renaissance influence, combined with inspiration from great French gardens of the time. The move away from heraldic to symbolic references was typical of a Renaissance garden and Theobalds boasted 'twelve Roman emperors in white marble'. In addition, a mount was planted with a maze or labyrinth, presenting visitors with a horticultural puzzle to negotiate before they could encounter Venus, the goddess of gardens as well as of love, at its centre. This desire to present intellectual challenges to visitors became a favourite device in Elizabethan gardens.

> One goes into the garden, encompassed with a
> ditch full of water, large enough to have the
> pleasure of going in a boat, and rowing between
> the shrubs; here are a variety of trees and
> plants; labyrinths made with a great deal of
> labour; a jet d'eau, with its basin of white marble;
> and columns and pyramids of wood, up and
> down the garden…

> *Travels in England and the Reign of Elizabeth*, Paul
> Hentzner, 1598

Other great Elizabethan houses and gardens were created around the country and, like Theobalds, they were designed to ensure they were fit to entertain royalty. Elizabeth I, unlike her father, saw no danger in allowing the wealthy to create magnificent homes and many noblemen aspired to accommodate the queen during her travels. The fashionable Elizabethan architect Robert Smythson designed Wollaton Hall in Nottinghamshire and his drawings detail the layout of the gardens, which had a more open plan than those at Theobalds. A painting by Jan Siberechts shows the garden in 1607 as a magnificent architectural creation with large open lawns, dramatic terraces and structural hedges, and rows of formally trained trees. A large fountain formed a focal point at the centre of three large square lawns dissected by paths.

Lord Lumley's work at Henry VIII's Nonsuch Palace had brought the gardens up to date and the palace became a favourite of Elizabeth I. The gardens were enclosed and were laid out still in the formal geometric fashion of early Tudor gardens. However, Lumley was an enthusiastic Renaissance man, having brought back ideas from his visit to Italy in 1566, so formal water features and stone statuary again played an important part, as described by a German visitor:

> In the pleasure and artificial gardens are many
> columns and pyramids of marble, two fountains

17th-century view of Wollaton Hall and Park by Jan Siberechts

that spout water, one round, the other a pyramid,
upon which are perched small birds that stream
water out of their bills.

The Tudor gardens at Hampton Court also continued to develop under the care of Elizabeth I. In 1599 Thomas Platter described the topiary in the late Elizabethan garden:

There were all manner of shapes, men and
women, half men and half horse, sirens, serving
maids with baskets, French lilies and delicate
crenellations all round made from dry twigs
bound together and the aforesaid evergreen
quick-set shrubs, or entirely of rosemary, all true
to the life, and so cleverly and amusingly
interwoven, mingled and grown together, trimmed
and arranged picture-wise that their equal would
be difficult to find.

Travels in England, Thomas Platter, 1599

Rosemary Verey's Elizabethan garden at Holdenby House in Northamptonshire

Robert Dudley, Earl of Leicester, created another important Elizabethan Renaissance-style garden at Kenilworth Castle in Warwickshire. He was a great favourite of Elizabeth I and, in 1575, held a water pageant with fireworks to mark her visit to the castle. There are suggestions that this event influenced

Reconstruction drawing of Kenilworth Castle in the Tudor period by Ivan Lapper

Shakespeare's *A Midsummer Night's Dream* and also Sir Walter Scott's novel *Kenilworth*. Attending the event was a court official, Robert Laneham, who wrote a letter that included detailed descriptions of the garden:

> …*There are also four equal parterres, cut in regular portions: in the middle of each is a post shaped like a cube, two feet high; on that a pyramid, accurately made, symmetrically carved, fifteen feet high; on the summit a ball ten inches in diameter, and the whole thing from top to*

*bottom, pedestal and all, hewn out of one solid
block of porphyry, and then much art and skill
brought here and set up. Flowering plants,
procured at great expense, yield sweet scent and
beauty, with fresh herbs and flowers, their colours
and their many kinds betraying a vast outlay;
then fruit trees full of apples, pears and ripe
cherries – a garden indeed so laid out that,
either on or above the lovely terrace paths, one
feels a refreshing breeze in the heat of summer,
or the pleasant cool of the fountain. One can
pluck from their stalks, and eat, fine strawberries
and cherries…*

The replica 17th-century knot garden at the Museum of Garden History in London

Knot gardens of the early Tudor period were simple devices that relied on hedges laid out in geometric patterns based on circles and squares or parts thereof. Box, *Buxus sempervirens*, was not a popular plant at this time and it is more likely that the hedges were planted with woody herbs like lavender, hyssop, marjoram and thyme. Simple flowering plants like pot marigold and violets were sometimes planted within the knot enclosures, but the gardens were more usually left bare, sometimes with coloured gravel, brick dust, chalk or grass providing carpets of colour. A large area of the main garden could be covered in a series of knots, each with a different pattern.

By the Elizabethan period, the love affair with the knot garden had really developed. Designs became ever more elaborate, although the knot patterns were usually contained within a square framework of the same hedge material. Knot designs were often symbolic, interlaced with hidden meanings. As patterns became more elaborate and intertwining, with a free style that was more flowing than the strictly geometric designs of earlier years, the link with embroidery and needlework can clearly be seen. These elaborate patterns were, like the earlier gardens, usually left unplanted within the internal compartments but simpler designs sometimes contained flowers.

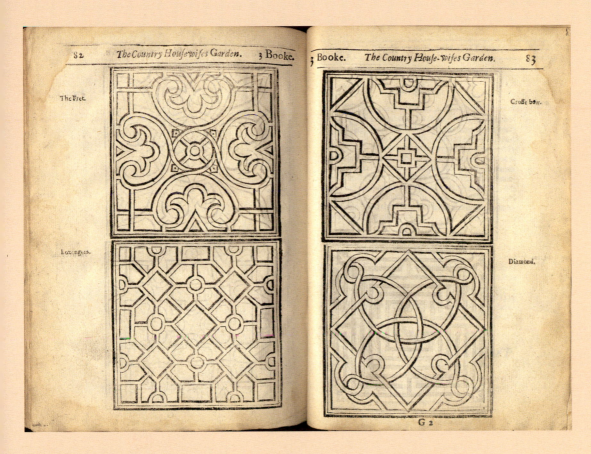

The Fret.

Crosse bow.

Lozenges.

Diamond.

G 2

Knot designs from William Lawson's The Country House-wifes Garden

The hedge of a knot garden created a perfect frame to enclose and exhibit the latest prized plant introduction. Some confusion is caused by the gradual use of the French name 'parterre' through the late 16th century, the meaning of which varies between a pattern on the ground, or an interwoven garden, but was often at this stage synonymous with knot garden. Mazes also became popular at this time, but these were only grown to a maximum knee height and were designed to present a puzzle to visitors.

By the early Stuart period, box – already favoured in France – was gaining popularity as a low hedging plant in Britain. Knot garden designs were published in William Lawson's *The Country House-wifes Garden* (1617) and Gervase Markham's *The Country Farm* (1616), indirectly translated from the French *Maison Rustique* (1586). The patterns were increasingly complex: for example the technique of weaving 'threads' of the hedge under and over itself became popular and there was less reliance on a square, enclosing framework.

A plan of the gardens – including knot designs – in front of a house from William Lawson's A New Orchard or Garden

Little Moreton Hall, Cheshire

Knot gardens of the mid- to late 17th century were more influenced by elaborate French design and the translation of the word 'parterre' developed into meaning an embroidered garden, or 'parterre de broderie'. Traditional, square-framed knot gardens were by this time considered old-fashioned and fell out of favour. Different plant material was used to create 'threads' of embroidery or, in the words of John Parkinson, 'trails'. It also became more common to plant flowering plants within the knot.

Partly due to Parkinson's writing, box became a more popular hedging plant and, with the strong Dutch influence on British gardens, other later 17th-century designs developed that accentuated a bold evergreen outline. The master of this craft was Leonard Meager, who published *The English Gardener* in 1670. One of his designs was used in the 1970s as inspiration for the gardens at Little Moreton Hall in Cheshire.

create a knot garden

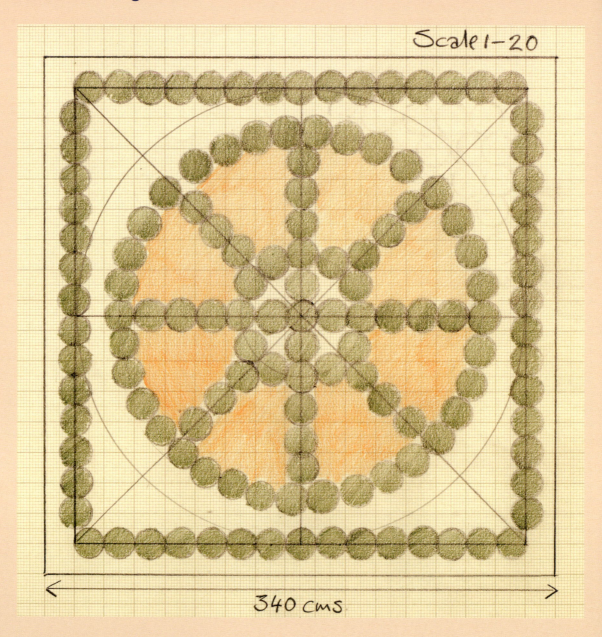

Scale 1–20

340 cms

Even the simplest knot garden can introduce style and sophistication to large and small gardens alike. They can be either traditional or contemporary in design and therefore adapt to both historic and modern settings.

The following instructions detail how to set out and plant a 10ft (3m) square knot garden within an area of established turf and will have to be adapted for different sizes and situations. Should you decide to try something larger or more complex, you should draw out the design to scale before transposing it onto the ground.

❖ Remove a section of turf approximately 11ft (3.40m) square, within which your 10ft (3m) square knot garden will sit centrally. The knot should sit square within the area you are working; for example parallel with a terrace or directly opposite the main door or window that overlooks the garden.

❖ Dig the soil down to a good spade depth and add in some organic matter, such as well-rotted farmyard manure or mushroom compost.

create a knot garden

❖ Level the ground by treading and raking two or three times across the area, changing direction each time.

❖ Set out string lines to form a 10ft (3m) square, 8in (200mm) in from each edge, then run diagonal string lines across from each corner.

❖ The point at which the lines cross is the centre of your square. Insert a garden cane at this point, attach a string to the cane and draw a circle into the soil that just touches the centre of each outside edge, as shown in the diagram above.

❖ These string lines and the circle scribed into the soil are your planting lines. Plant dwarf box, lavender, rosemary or other woody herbs between 6 and 8in (150 and 200mm) apart along the guidelines and you will form the juvenile pattern of your knot garden.

Over the next season or two the plants will grow and join up to form the solid lines of a knot garden hedge. For the first few years you will need to encourage the plants to become bushy as well as tall, so you should cut back approximately two-thirds of the new growth in late spring each year. Once the hedge has reached the height you desire, simply clip it to the same framework each year. Woody herbs might need one or two light haircuts through summer to keep the knot garden tidy.

❖ You could also top dress the soil with coloured gravel or stone chippings in Tudor style. Plants like lavender look effective inside the hedge.

Stuart Gardens

The Jacobean style of architecture, which developed between 1603 and 1649, was a major influence on garden design during the Stuart period. Jacobean houses were characterised by elaborate decoration on plasterwork, brickwork and joinery, and the relationship between house and garden and the architectural quality of the latter became increasingly important. As in the Elizabethan period, Jacobean country houses were built on a lavish scale, fit to entertain royalty. A fine example was the magnificent Audley End in Essex, built for Thomas Howard, 1st Earl of Suffolk, which was surrounded by a great formal garden that incorporated avenues of trees, formal ponds and wide walkways or alleys.

This period sees the increasing involvement of the architect in garden design and this trend continued to be an essential element of garden development in the 18th century. Jacobean architects, like Inigo Jones (1573–1652), continued to be inspired by Italy, but also increasingly by French design. Jones worked with the French garden designer and engineer Isaac de Caus (1590–1648) on the gardens at Wilton House near Salisbury, which were designed to incorporate a range of elaborate water features. One of the most notable was a large rectangular pool decorated with fountains, one of which was in the form of a rotating crown that sent out jets of water from its elevated position on top of a stone column.

'[A garden is a] place of all terrestriall enjoyments the most resembling Heaven, and the best representation of our lost felicitie…'

Round-headed leek, Allium sphaercephalon

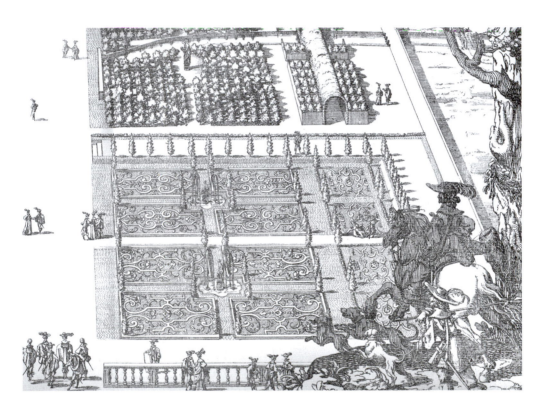

Isaac and his brother Salomon (1576–1626), a hydraulic engineer, were important figures in British garden design, known primarily for their ambitious water projects. The elaborate use of water in gardens became increasingly popular through Elizabeth I's reign and continued into the Jacobean period. The combination of aesthetics with science used in these complex installations is the perfect demonstration of true Renaissance influence on British garden design at this time.

A bird's eye view of the gardens designed by Isaac de Caus at Wilton House, Wiltshire

Isaac de Caus's design for a water feature at Wilton House

Like Inigo Jones, Salomon de Caus also worked for Anne of Denmark, the wife of James I, at Somerset House. Here a raised walkway and terraces looked down upon a geometrically laid out, symmetrical garden. Steps led down to this area and linked with four central paths forming a cross. Other features included avenues of trees, classical statues and a grotto, all reflecting new fashions in England inspired by Renaissance garden design and French formal garden styles.

create a topiary

lower leaves removed

Topiary can be developed in two main ways: either by training a young cutting to grow as a single stem, straight and long up a cane, or by cutting into a mature shrub. Many woody, evergreen plants can be used to create a piece of topiary; traditionally species like box, yew and bay are used. However, woody herbs also make an effective miniature topiary that develops quickly into the finished specimen. These instructions show you how to develop a rosemary lollipop from a cutting. The same basic rules and principles apply to other suitable plant material.

❖ In August take 4in (100mm) long semi-ripe cuttings from an established rosemary plant, *Rosmarinus officinalis*. (Semi-ripe wood is one season's growth which is just beginning to turn woody.) Peel the shoots gently from the plant to create a 'heel' of older wood.

❖ Carefully remove the lower leaves from the cutting, to avoid contact with the soil.

❖ Fill 3.5in (90mm) pots with a gritty, well-drained compost (for example 50/50 soil-based compost mixed with horticultural sand or perlite), taking care to firm the compost. Using a fine dibber or slim pencil, make holes in the firmed compost and insert a cutting, firming the compost back around the stem. Up to eight cuttings can be placed into a 3.5in (90mm) pot.

Put the pots in a cold frame or unheated greenhouse; in mild areas you could even leave them outside, sheltered from the worst of the weather and out of direct sunlight. Ensure the compost does not dry out completely, but otherwise you do not need to do anything until the following spring.

By March or April the cuttings should have rooted and each can be potted into individual 3.5in (90mm) pots with fresh compost. Insert a slim cane right next to each cutting and gently tie the two together using soft garden twine.

Throughout this growing season, train the young plant straight up the cane by tying in extension growth regularly.

As the upright growth develops, the lower side shoots should gradually be nipped off to ensure alternative leaders do not develop, but leave some of the higher shoots and leaves in place.

Once the young plant reaches the required height, perhaps 14in (350mm) for a rosemary lollipop, pinch out the vertical, leading shoot. This encourages side shoots to grow and gradually you can begin to develop the lollipop head over a period of two or three years.

Continually nip out the growth to create a denser head. As this develops, all lower, unwanted shoots and leaves can be removed until you finally create the mature lollipop head topiary. Follow this simple process for a variety of plants and shapes, adapting it to create espaliers or fans by using different supports.

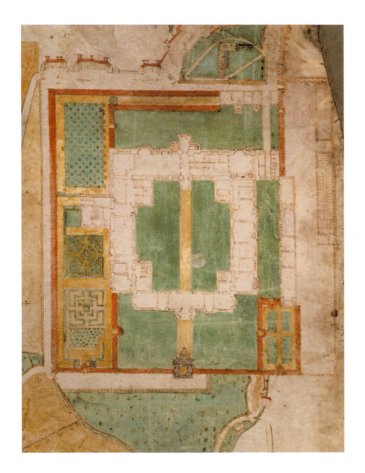

A 1608 plan of the early gardens at Hatfield House

One of the most important houses and gardens of the Jacobean period was Hatfield House in Hertfordshire where Salomon de Caus was eventually to take responsibility for the water features. The Old Palace at Hatfield was acquired by Robert Cecil, 1st Earl of Salisbury, when his previous home at

View of the foot maze at Hatfield House

Theobalds, a few miles to the south, caught the attention of King James I. As was the way of things at the time, the king soon took ownership of the modern house and gardens at Theobalds, and Cecil had to begin work building a new house at Hatfield to replace the old-fashioned 15th-century manor house. In 1607 building work began on the Jacobean house and Cecil also turned his attention to the surrounding land where he planned to make magnificent gardens. With the help of the gardener John Tradescant the Elder, the gardens were

Newel carving from the Grand Staircase at Hatfield House, possibly depicting John Tradescant the Elder

laid out and planted over the next five years, overseen by Mountain Jennings, Cecil's gardener from Theobalds. Salomon de Caus built the elaborate French-inspired water gardens below the main terrace, from where they could be viewed and these included a huge marble basin filled with rock supporting a copper-coloured statue that formed the centrepiece, with streams of water surrounding it.

Beyond de Caus's work, the formal gardens developed as a series of terraces leading down from the house. The Tudor

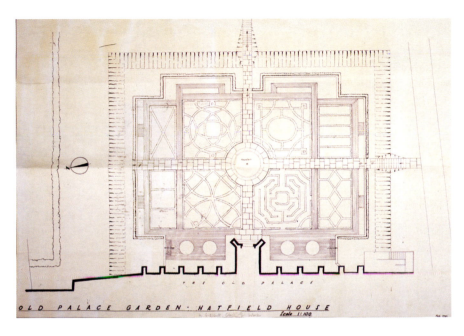

OLD PALACE GARDEN · HATFIELD HOUSE
Scale 1:100

tradition of parallel walks, knots, and avenues of trees continued, but the planting at Hatfield was to be at the leading edge of Jacobean horticulture. Tradescant travelled to Europe to bring back all manner of plants, including fruit trees, flowering plants and bulbs for the new gardens. Rare specimens were sent as gifts to Robert Cecil and the wife of the French Ambassador to England, Madame de la Broderie, sent 30,000 vines. The gardens were seen as significant at the time and, thanks to the re-creation of the Jacobean-style gardens by the Dowager Marchioness of Salisbury over the last 30 years, remain so today.

Lady Salisbury's 1981 design for the knot garden at Hatfield House

The Dowager Marchioness's gardens at Hatfield House today reflect the character of the original ones seen by Monsieur de Sorbiere c 1663

Monsieur de Sorbiere, a visitor to Hatfield *c* 1663, described the gardens:

> …*We Dined in a Hall that looked into a Greenplot with Two Fountains in it, and having Espaliers on the Sides, but a Balister before it, upon which are Flower-Pots and Statues: From this Parterre there is a way down by Two Pairs of Stairs, of about twelve or Fifteen Steps to another…From this Terrass you have a Prospect of the great water Parterre I have spoken of…*

The Spring Garden from **Hortus Floridus** *(1614–15) by Crispin I de Passe*

Inigo Jones remained popular with the monarchy and, in 1639, was commissioned by Charles I to develop Wimbledon House — previously owned by the Cecil family — for his wife, Henrietta Maria. The French designer André Mollet (d 1665) was also commissioned to update the Wimbledon gardens in 1639, but Henrietta Maria was never to see them; by the time the gardens were completed she had fled to Holland to escape the aftermath of the English Civil War. During the

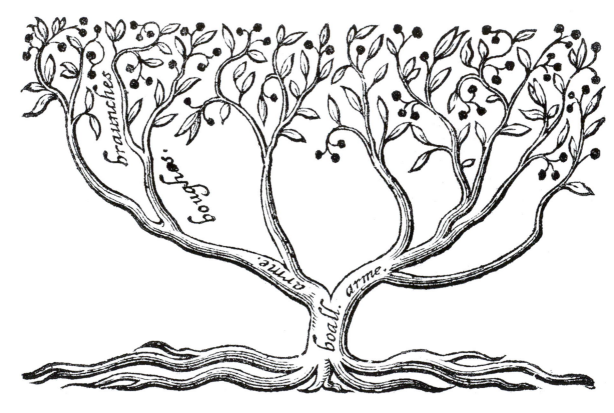

The perfect forme of a Fruit-tree.

'The perfect forme of a Fruit-tree' from William Lawson's
A New Orchard or Garden

Elizabethan period, the gardens at Wimbledon followed the fashion of the time and were laid out as a series of small individual gardens, each enclosed by a hedge or wall, and laid out in different knots and topiary. Under Mollet's direction this earlier design was opened up to allow vistas through the central area and the newly fashionable symmetry was introduced. In typical French style there were large numbers of citrus trees, planted in tubs and laid out in a formal pattern throughout the Orange Garden in summer, before being carried inside for protection in winter. Four knot gardens were laid out and, indicative of the growing interest in plants, were designed so that flowers could be grown within the hedge compartments. Box was used for the hedging, a species that had not been popular in Elizabethan gardens as its smell was considered offensive.

Late Stuart gardens

During the late Stuart period garden designers expanded their horizons, both literally and metaphorically. The enclosed gardens of the later medieval and Tudor periods were already being gradually opened up through the early Stuart years and this was to become a more exaggerated aspect of late 17th-century garden design. Views, vistas and distant focal points became increasingly important as did the relationship between house and garden, the scale and proportion of the two and the creation of a series of different axes radiating from the house and immediate surroundings. This sense of space and perspective reflects elements of the baroque, a style already popular in France, Spain and Italy and quickly reaching Holland, Germany and Britain.

The North Prospect of Hampton Court *(c 1699) by Leonard Knyff*

Once Charles II was restored to the British throne following the Civil War, horticultural activity resumed. With a king who had been shown hospitality in France during his exile, it is easy to understand why André Mollet would have been popular with Charles II and, by 1661, he was the King's Gardener at St James's Palace. Here Mollet was responsible for introducing a large canal surrounded by walks radiating out from a semicircle of trees, known as *patte d'oie*, and the following year he was invited to create similar, but somewhat grander, features at Hampton Court where almost 800 lime trees were planted.

The Park, formerly a flat, naked piece of Ground, now planted with sweete rows of lime-trees, and the Canale for water now neere perfected.

Elysium Britannicum, John Evelyn

Topiary at Levens Hall, Cumbria. The gardens at Levens Hall were originally laid out in the late 17th-century by Monsieur Guillaume Beaumont, a former pupil of André Le Nôtre.

Charles II was an ambitious garden-maker and he soon turned his attention from Hampton Court to Greenwich Palace and to another great French landscape designer, André Le Nôtre (1613–1700). Le Nôtre had recently created beautifully proportioned gardens on a grand scale at Château de Vaux le

Vicomte near Paris. He also designed a large parterre for the Renaissance gardens at the Château de Fontainebleau and was about to commence extensive work at Versailles. Consequently, and not surprisingly, Le Nôtre was too busy to visit Greenwich so he sent his ambitious plans to England for execution. Although an enormous number of trees were planted to create formal avenues and dramatic earth-moving work was carried out to create levels, terraces and steps, there was insufficient money to complete the design, which would have included elaborate parterres and fountains.

During the reign of William and Mary, gardens began to incorporate various elements found in Dutch garden design, including an emphasis on formality and the use of large canals and dramatic avenues of trees. These features, combined with the strong French influence introduced earlier by Charles II, saw a gradual change in 17th-century garden design that would eventually develop into the English Landscape Movement of the mid-18th century.

There was one substantial difference between England and Holland that would make the transference of Dutch garden styles rather difficult. The low-lying flatlands of the Netherlands were ideal for expansive formal gardens with their long straight canals, avenues of trees and large elaborate parterres. Creating the same style of garden in Britain often meant

The formal parterres of the Privy Garden at Hampton Court

investing in expensive earth moving, which was not without difficulty and could result in problems such as poor drainage in the future. Gardens with these features could also look extremely contrived in the British landscape, with the large level plains looking incongruous set among more hilly terrain.

The planting and layout of the restored Privy Garden at Hampton Court clearly evidences William and Mary's Dutch influence

Therefore, during the Stuart period, British gardens developed in the form of a hybrid that brought together the lasting inheritance from Italian Renaissance gardens, first developed during the Tudor period, with fashionable ideas from grand French gardens and the new influence of large, elegant Dutch

Ham House, Richmond

gardens. Added to this already complex melting pot was the occasional English invention such as the *parterre à l'Anglaise*, the English parterre, where turf was cut into intricate patterns, interspersed by gravel paths. From the mid- to late 17th century such composite gardens were made in Britain at Wilton House in Wiltshire, Ragley Hall in Warwickshire and Hadham Hall in Hertfordshire. Although these no longer exist, the National Trust have recreated 17th-century style gardens at Ham House in Surrey.

An important horticultural partnership developed in the late 17th century, which played an important role in the transition from formal 17th-century gardens to the more open designs of the early 18th century. George London (fl 1681–1714) was an established garden designer and a partner in the famous Brompton Park Nursery in Kensington by the time he set up in partnership with horticulturalist Henry Wise (1653–1738) in 1689. The nursery then became known as London & Wise and became the most fashionable and influential establishment to commission for the design, execution and planting of a modern, late Stuart garden. The earlier Brompton Park Nursery partnership, in which Moses Cook worked with London, had already played an important part in the creation of significant gardens such as Longleat in Wiltshire and Chatsworth in Derbyshire.

London worked for William and Mary in an official capacity and was responsible for continuing Charles II's improvements to the gardens at Hampton Court in 1690. Several thousand more lime trees were planted in dense avenues, some four rows deep, and an enormous parterre garden was laid out as an intricate embroidery of turf intersected with weaving paths of coloured gravel in the style of an English parterre. London then went on to work at William and Mary's private residence in Kensington; by the following year he had established more parterres and avenues in Kensington gardens, which was conveniently close to his nursery. Wise was originally London's apprentice but eventually became his business partner. He was Royal Gardener to Queen Anne and George I and was responsible for designing and laying out several important late 17th- and early 18th-century gardens, including Kensington Gardens and Blenheim Palace.

Sneezewort 'The Pearl', Achillea ptarmica *The Pearl Group*

Plants

The ports of Tudor and Stuart England were exciting places, with merchants bringing in new and exotic merchandise from all over the world. Prior to this period, imports were only seen from Europe and parts of Asia, but in the early to mid-16th century North and South America were being explored and, in 1577, Sir Francis Drake began his circumnavigation of the world. Therefore, from the late-16th century, all manner of goods, including plants and exotic fruits, were shipped to Britain where wealthy, educated Tudors eagerly purchased them for planting in their newly laid out gardens. Important introductions from the Tudor and Stuart period include the sunflower, *Helianthus annuus* (1596), Cedar of Lebanon, *Cedrus libani* (c 1630), banana, *Musa x paradisiaca* (1633) and sweet pea, *Lathyrus odoratus* (1670).

The garden historian has a range of sources from which to extract information about plants of the Tudor and Stuart period, although accurate identification can often be a problem. It was not until the 18th century that Carl Linnaeus (1707–78) invented the plant nomenclature that remains in use today; records from earlier years use less scientific systems for naming plants. This is clearly seen in the plant lists produced by the John Tradescants in the 17th century. For example their lists record *Sedum acre*, or stonecrop, as '*Illecebra minor acris*' and the white wallflower, *Erysimum cheiri*

The Crown Imperial for his stately beautifulness, deserveth the first place in this our garden of delight.

Paradisi in Sole Paradisus Terrestris, John Parkinson, 1629

Sunflower, Helianthus annuus, *introduced in 1596 from North America*

73

(previously known as *Cheiranthus*), as *'Keiri flore albo simplex'*. Nevertheless, with the aid of such lists and books of the time and thanks to the expertise of plant and garden historians in translating names, there is a wealth of information about the different species grown in Britain during this period.

Although monks had produced herbals for centuries, garden books and what were in effect plant encyclopaedias became more widely available during the Elizabethan period. Dr William Turner (1508–68), a churchman and naturalist, published what is thought to have been the first herbal written in the English language in 1551, with the second part published in 1562 and the third and final volume in 1568. The book was titled *A New Herbal* and Turner became known as the 'Father of English Botany'.

One of the most famous herbals, still in print today, is John Gerard's *The Herbal or General History of Plants*, first published in 1597. Gerard (1545–c 1611) was gardener to Lord Burleigh at Theobalds in Hertfordshire and London for 20 years and the gardens under his care were typical of the Elizabethan period when the wealthy grew a wide variety of fashionable, newly introduced plants. Gerard also made his own garden in Holborn, London and, being well connected in the horticultural world, received many 'new' plants that he was able to grow and then write about. His book was a

Page of floral drawings from Florilegium

Opposite: **Two woodcuts from John Gerard's** The Herbal or General History of Plants: *the box tree,* **Buxus sempervirens,** *and the Anemone of Constantinople,* **Anemone latifolia**

combination of folklore, plant descriptions, uses and cultivation requirements and each plant was illustrated with a woodcut image, totalling just under 2,000 in total. Thomas Johnson improved the book in 1633 and it is this edition that has stood the test of time.

> These Gillofloures, especially the Carnations, are
> kept in pots in the extremitie of our cold
> Winters. The Clove Gillofloure endureth better the
> cold, and therefore is planted in gardens. They
> flourish and floure most part of the Summer…
> The conserve made of the floures of the Clove
> Gillofloure and sugar, is exceeding cordiall, and
> wonderfully above measure doth comfort the
> heart, being eaten now and then.

The Herbal or General History of Plants, John Gerard
(Thomas Johnson's edition), 1633

As gardeners began to look at plants as much for their aesthetic qualities as for their healing properties, the emphasis gradually changed from recording them solely for their uses, to including information about their ornamental attributes. John Parkinson's (1567–1650) *Paradisi in Sole Paradisus Terrestris* (translated as the 'terrestrial paradise of the park in the sun') was published in 1629 and is generally recognised as the first of this genre.

The John Tradescants

Parkinson was a contemporary and friend of the John Tradescants – royal gardeners, plant collectors, nurserymen and museum owners – and it is to them we turn to trace the origins of the British obsession for collecting and growing non-native plants. Foreign species had arrived in Britain from as far back as the Roman invasion, but it was in the Tudor period that wealthy men first commissioned long, expensive and often hazardous journeys for the sole reason of bringing new ornamental plants into the country.

John Tradescant the Elder (1570–1638) was one of the first of these gardeners-cum-explorers, and his son, John the Younger (1608–62), was to follow in his footsteps. Although many of

Left: *17th-century portrait of John Tradescant the Elder, attributed to Emanuel de Critz*

Right: *17th-century portrait of John Tradescant the Younger with Roger Friend, attributed to Thomas de Critz*

the plants they introduced are often difficult to identify today, or may not even be considered garden-worthy, the Tradescant's play a vital part in British garden history. In addition to bringing new plants into the country themselves, they moved in fashionable gardening circles and swapped specimens with other collectors and enthusiasts. They eventually created an important garden and nursery in Lambeth where all manner of new plants were grown, including the herb angelica, *Angelica archangelica*, introduced by John Tradescant the Elder. Among his son's introductions are the tulip tree, *Liriodendron tulipifera*, and a form of yucca, *Yucca filamentosa*. The plant that bears their name, *Tradescantia virginiana,* was in fact given to the Tradescants by a friend who collected it in Virginia.

John Tradescant the Elder was gardener to Robert Cecil at Hatfield House in Hertfordshire from 1610 and was responsible for continuing the development of the gardens around the Jacobean house. By the autumn of 1610, Tradescant was sent on his first journey to Europe to purchase plants, particularly fruit trees and vines. One bill from Holland includes varieties of medlar, pear, quince, cherries, apples and white currants, and another lists mulberries, lime trees and red currants. Ornamental plants purchased by Tradescant included roses, anemones, daphne, fritillaries and the jonquil, a form of daffodil.

John Tradescant the Elder's bill for plants bought in Holland in 1612 for Hatfield House

Over the next few years, Tradescant was kept busy with more plant-buying expeditions as well as caring for Cecil's gardens at Hatfield, Cranborne in Dorset and the Strand in London. In 1615, after Cecil's death, Tradescant left Hatfield to work in Canterbury from where he travelled to Russia, collecting a range of plants including the false hellebore, *Veratrum album*, and a rose that is thought to have been *Rosa acicularis*, the prickly rose. He then moved on to work for the influential George Villiers, 1st Duke of Buckingham, of whom he became a trusted and loyal friend.

Tradescant rose up the social ladder and, by the late 1620s, was financially secure and able to take a lease on a house in semi-rural Lambeth, which he called The Ark. It had a small garden and an additional acre of land together with a 2-acre orchard; it was here that he established a museum in which he displayed the 'rareities and curiosities' collected on his travels. He also developed a garden, which according to a catalogue produced in 1634 contained over 700 different plant species. While developing his own gardens he was appointed royal gardener to Charles I in 1630, with the impressive title 'Keeper of the Gardens, Vines and Silkworms at Oatlands Palace'.

John Tradescant the Younger had been well educated and followed his father into a horticultural career. And, indeed, on his father's death he took over the position of royal

Common spiderwort, Tradescantia virginiana, *introduced in 1629 from North America and named in honour of the two John Tradescants*

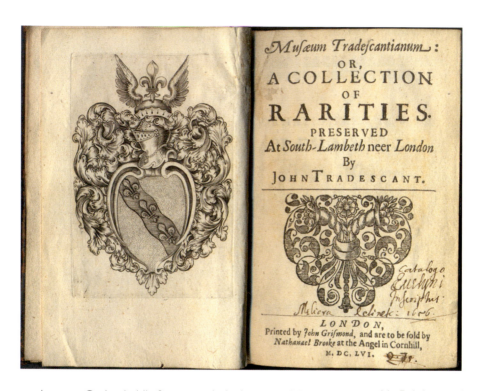

John Evelyn's personal copy of Musaeum Tradescantianum, *dated in his hand 1656. This book catalogued the Tradescants' museum collection at The Ark.*

gardener at Oatlands. His first recorded trip was to Virginia in 1638 at the king's request 'to gather up all raritye of flowers, plants, shells etc' and he returned to the colony in 1642. Tradescant the Younger clearly loved botanising and collecting and, as well as bringing many new plants back to Britain, continued to develop the collection at The Ark. Sea journeys took several months and many of Tradescant's plants died on board ship because of salt spray and lack of fresh water before reaching British shores. Many of the seeds rotted or were eaten by vermin on board ship. Some 50 years later diarist John Evelyn offered advice for increasing the survival rates of plants on such journeys:

> …seeds are best preserv'd in papers; their names written on them and put in a box. The Nutts in Barills of dry sand; each kind wraped in papers written on. The trees in Barills their rootes wraped about with mosse: The smaller the plants and trees are, the better; or they will do well packed up in matts; but the Barill is best & a small vessel will containe enough of all kinds with labels of paper tyed to every sort with ye name.

Monkshood, Aconitum napellus

Parrot tulips growing in the knot garden at the Museum of Garden History in London

As international trade developed, Holland became an important commercial centre and a wide range of merchandise, including plants and bulbs, passed through her ports, to be bought and sold by traders. The country became an important centre for commercial horticulture and continues to be so today. The tulip is often associated with Holland, where it is cultivated and propagated on a massive scale, and the flower best demonstrates the 17th-century fascination with 'new' or rare plants.

Between 1634 and 1637 a near hysterical obsession developed around the cultivation and acquisition of tulips, with those displaying streaked and feathered petals most popular. A rare and now extinct form called *Tulipa* 'Semper Augustus' with red and white petals was one of the most famous and much coveted. Today a rare raspberry and white tulip called *Tulipa* 'Zomerschoon' that originates from 1620 is still in cultivation although difficult to acquire; the nearest equivalent forms we can easily buy today are the extravagant parrot tulips such as *Tulipa* 'Flaming Parrot'.

It was not until the last century that botanists understood why a tulip bulb would suddenly, one spring, produce streaked or 'broken' petals, rather than plain ones. It was discovered that aphid activity on the leaves and flowers introduces a virus into the plant that travels to the bulb and affects the flower the following year.

Still Life with Basket and Vase of Flowers *by Jan Brueghel the Younger*

The unpredictability of the process and the random flower ornamentation that results fuelled a 17th-century fever that became known as 'Tulipomania'. Wealthy men became excited, not only at the prospect of acquiring an exquisite flower, but also perhaps at the risk associated with its purchase. It was in effect a form of gambling, for who could know whether the flower produced the following year would disappoint, live up to or even exceed the purchaser's expectation? The stakes were high: records show that men became bankrupt in their obsession to purchase a rare bulb and that houses, carriages and enormous amounts of money were exchanged at the height of the mania.

While the 'fever' was most prevalent in Holland, 'Tulipomania' also hit Britain and tulips became the 'must have' flowers for the fashionable late Tudor and Stuart garden. One indication of how widespread and influential the fashion was throughout Europe can be seen in the large number of still life images of the period, where beautiful tulips are shown either as single specimens or as collections displayed in vases and other containers.

Botanic studies

The increasing interest in plants was not purely aesthetic, nor was it specific to Britain. A fascination for science fuelled interest in botanical studies and the world's first botanic gardens, linked to universities, were established in Padua and Pisa in Italy in the mid-16th century, with Leiden's botanic garden in Holland created in the last years of the century. These gardens were originally made to assist in the scientific study of plants and most were not open to the public. The first British botanic garden opened in 1620 in Oxford, with Edinburgh following in 1670. The Royal Botanic Gardens at Kew were not established until the mid-18th century and Cambridge opened its botanic garden as late as the 19th century.

Plants had been used for centuries for their medicinal qualities, but, thanks to an increasing understanding of botany and the human body in general, a more scientific approach was gradually being applied to medicine. However, basic plant medicine remained important and ancient folklore and treatments were often still followed. Nicholas Culpepper (1616–54), like many Stuarts, was inspired by the work of classic academics and referred to and translated such ancient works.

Purple sage, Salvia officinalis 'Purpurascens'

A decoction of the leaves and branches of Sage made and drunk, saith Dioscorides, provokes urine and causeth the hair to become black. It stayeth the bleeding of wounds and cleaneth ulcers and sores. Three spoonsful of the juice of Sage taken fasting with a little honey arrests spitting or vomiting of blood in consumption. It is profitable for all pains in the head coming of cold rheumatic humours, as also for all pains in the joints, whether inwardly or outwardly. The juice of Sage in warm water cureth hoarseness and cough. Pliny saith it cureth stinging and biting serpents.

The English Physician, Nicholas Culpepper, 1652

The continuing reliance on natural cures is demonstrated by the fact that the only hope to ward off plague during the 17th-century outbreaks was to hold a posy of flowers to the nose. This custom is still practised by judges on ceremonial occasions today and is recorded in a children's playground song:

Ring a Ring o' Roses,
A pocketful of posies,
Atishoo! Atishoo!
We all fall down!

In 1665 the worst outbreak of bubonic plague hit London and it was only the disastrous Great Fire of London that finally controlled it the following year.

16th-century woodcut by Hans Weiditz the Younger depicting the growing of medicinal herbs in a herbal garden

Florists' societies

An increasing understanding of botany meant that by the 17th century, plants were propagated more reliably and, for the first time, there was an attempt to improve upon nature by encouraging double flowers or larger blooms to develop. Flowers that were considered to have special qualities were selected for specific propagation, using methods such as division or cuttings. Seeds were also collected, although at this time the sexual characteristics of plants were not understood and, as we know today, identical plants cannot be guaranteed from seed-grown stock. Interesting forms of plants would have occasionally been seen when garden plants crossed with one another, resulting in a natural hybrid; this would have caused great excitement among horticulturalists of the day.

The term 'florist' began to appear in the early decades of the 17th century, for example in John Parkinson's *Paradisus*. Unlike today a florist was not a person who sold cut flowers, but someone who grew certain plant species, purely for their aesthetic qualities. Societies were formed and enthusiasts would meet and exchange plants. By the mid-17th century there were four important florists' flowers: carnation, tulip, anemone and ranunculus. These were joined some years later by auriculas and other plants. Florists became very excited by flowers with multi-coloured petals, like some tulips, and those with double flowers or botanical oddities like 'hen and chickens' and 'hose-in-hose' forms.

The florists' movement grew throughout the following centuries with specific periodicals and flower shows developing. Even today long established horticultural clubs and societies, especially in the north of England, maintain the centuries old tradition in the way they propagate, distribute and display florists' flowers.

Lady tulip 'Cynthia', Tulipa clusiana 'Cynthia', known to John Parkinson as 'the early Persian tulip'

The following lists of plants, while not exhaustive, gives an indication of plants that were available in Tudor and Stuart Britain. All the plants listed are available in one form or another, whether as seed, container-grown plants or, in the case of some woodier plants, bare-rooted trees and shrubs. If you want to plant a reproduction Tudor garden you might find that some of the plants are not readily available in their simple forms. Often a plant like masterwort, *Astrantia major*, will be available in garden centres as a range of modern hybrids. It is crucial then to decide whether your planting must be authentic or whether it is to be 'in the style of' Tudor and Stuart planting, in which case you will have a wider palette to select from and will find the plants easier to obtain.

Many cultivated forms of plants are only available as container-grown specimens because they are often propagated vegetatively (eg as cuttings or by layering). However, most annuals and many British wild flowers, native or naturalised, are rarely sold in garden centres as established plants because they are short-lived and uneconomical to grow on a commercial scale. Your only option will be to grow them from seed from specialist suppliers.

Please remember that under the Wildlife and Countryside Act it is illegal to uproot any wild plant and to take material from protected species. All the plants listed in this book are available from legitimate sources.

BOTANICAL NAME	COMMON NAME	PLANTS	SEED

Annuals, biennials and perennials

BOTANICAL NAME	COMMON NAME	PLANTS	SEED
Achillea ptarmica The Pearl Group	Sneezewort 'The Pearl''	Widely available	Available
Adonis aestivalis	Summer adonis	Unusual	Available
Acanthus mollis	Bear's breeches	Widely available	Available
Acanthus spinosus	Armed bear's breeches	Widely available	Available
Achillea millefolium	Common yarrow	Available	Widely available
Aconitum napellus	Monkshood	Widely available	Available
Alcea rosea	Hollyhock	Available	Available
Alchemilla conjuncta	Silver Lady's mantle	Widely available	Unusual
Aquilegia canadensis	Akaly	Available	Widely available
Aquilegia vulgaris	Common columbine	Available	Widely available
Argemone mexicana	Prickly poppy	Available	Available
Armeria maritima	Thrift	Available	Available
Asphodeline lutea	Yellow asphodel	Widely available	Available
Astrantia major	Great black masterwort	Widely available	Available
Calendula officinalis	Common marigold	Available	Widely available
Campanula glomerata	Clustered bellflower	Available	Available
Campanula persicifolia	Peach-leaved bellflower	Widely available	Available
Cerinthe major	Honeywort	Available	Available
Consolida ajacis	Larkspur	Available	Available
Convallaria majalis	Lily of the valley	Widely available	Available
Dianthus 'Painted Lady'	Old-fashioned pink	Available	Unusual
Dianthus 'Sops-in-Wine'	Old-fashioned pink	Available	Unusual
Dictamnus albus	Dittany	Widely available	Available
Digitalis lutea	Small yellow foxglove	Widely available	Available

Great black masterwort, Astrantia major

Tree *lavatera*, Lavatera olbia

BOTANICAL NAME	COMMON NAME	PLANTS	SEED
Digitalis purpurea	Common foxglove	🌱	🟢 🟢
Dryopteris filix-mas	Male fern	🌱	N/A
Echium vulgare	Viper's bugloss	🌱	🟢
Euphorbia lathyris	Caper spurge	🌱	🟢
Euphorbia palustris	Marsh spurge	🌱 🌱	🟢
Filipendula ulmaria	Meadow sweet	🌱 🌱	🟢 🟢
Galega officinalis	Common goat's rue	🌱 🌱	🟢
Geranium macrorrhizum	Rock cranesbill	🌱 🌱	🟢
Geranium phaeum	Mourning widow	🌱 🌱	🟢
Geranium sanguineum	Bloody cranesbill	🌱 🌱	🟢
Geranium versicolor	Pencilled geranium	🌱 🌱	🟢
Glaucium flavum	Horned poppy	🌱	🟢
Helianthus annuus	Sunflower	🌱	🟢 🟢
Helleborus foetidus	Stinking hellebore	🌱 🌱	🟢
Helleborus niger	Christmas rose	🌱 🌱	🟢
Helleborus orientalis	Lenten rose	🌱	🟢
Hemerocallis lilioasphodelus (H. flava)	Yellow day lily	🌱 🌱	🟢
Hemerocallis fulva	Common orange day lily	🌱	🟢
Hesperis matronalis	Sweet rocket	🌱 🌱	🟢 🟢
Lunaria annua	Annual honesty	🌱	🟢 🟢
Lunaria rediviva	Perennial honesty	🌱	🟢
Lychnis chalcedonica	Maltese cross	🌱 🌱	🟢 🟢
Lychnis coronaria	Rose campion	🌱 🌱	🟢 🟢
Musa × paradisiaca	Common banana	Cultivars only	🟢
Paeonia mascula	English/coral peony	🌱	🟢

BOTANICAL NAME	COMMON NAME	PLANTS	SEED
Polemonium caeruleum	Jacob's ladder	🪴🪴	◆ ◆
Primula auricula	Auricula	🪴	◆
Primula veris	Common cowslip	🪴🪴	◆ ◆
Primula vulgaris	Primrose	🪴🪴	◆ ◆
Pulmonaria officinalis	Common lungwort	🪴	◆
Pulsatilla vulgaris	Pasqueflower	🪴🪴	◆ ◆
Rudbeckia laciniata	Cut-leaved coneflower	🪴	◆
Tradescantia virginiana	Common spiderwort	🪴	◆
Viola odorata	Sweet violet	🪴🪴	◆ ◆
Viola tricolor	Heart's ease	🪴	◆ ◆

Bulbs and tubers

BOTANICAL NAME	COMMON NAME	PLANTS	SEED
Allium moly	Yellow garlic	🪴	◆
Allium sphaerocephalon	Round-headed leek	🪴🪴	◆
Anemone nemorosa	Wood anemone	🪴🪴	◆
Anthericum liliago	St Bernard's lily	🪴	◆
Asphodelus albus	White-flowered asphodel	🪴	◆
Colchicum autumnale	Meadow saffron	🪴	◆
Dracunculus vulgaris	Dragon arum	🪴	◆
Eranthis hyemalis	Winter aconite	🪴	◆
Erythronium dens-canis	Dog's tooth violet	🪴🪴	◆
Fritillaria imperialis	Crown imperial	🪴	◆
Fritillaria meleagris	Snake's head fritillary	🪴🪴	◆
Fritillaria persica	Persian lily	🪴	◆
Geranium tuberosum	Tuberous-rooted cranesbill	🪴	◆
Gladiolus communis subsp. byzantinus	Byzantine gladiolus	🪴🪴	◆

Peach-leaved bellflower, Campanula persicifolia

Common goat's rue, Galega officinalis

BOTANICAL NAME	COMMON NAME	PLANTS	SEED
Iris germanica	Bearded iris	🪴	◆
Iris foetidissima	Stinking iris	🪴 🪴	◆
Leucojum aestivum	Summer snowflake	🪴	◆
Lilium candidum	Madonna lily	🪴	◆
Lilium martagon	Turk's cap lily	🪴 🪴	◆
Mirabilis jalapa	Marvel of Peru	🪴	◆ ◆
Narcissus pseudonarcissus	Wild daffodil	🪴	◆
Narcissus triandrus	Angel's tears	🪴	◆
Polygonatum × hybridum	Solomon's seal	🪴 🪴	◆
Tulipa clusiana	Lady tulip	🪴	◆
Tulipa sylvestris	Wild tulip	🪴	◆

Herbs

Allium schoenoprasum	Chives	🪴 🪴	◆ ◆
Angelica archangelica	Angelica	🪴 🪴	◆ ◆
Artemisia abrotanum	Southernwood	🪴 🪴	◆
Borago officinalis	Borage	🪴	◆ ◆
Chamaemelum nobile	Chamomile	🪴	◆ ◆
Fragaria moschata	Hautbois	🪴	◆
Fragaria vesca	Wild strawberry	🪴	◆
Galium odoratum	Sweet woodruff	🪴 🪴	◆
Helichrysum italicum	Curry plant	🪴 🪴	◆
Hyssopus officinalis	Hyssop	🪴 🪴	◆ ◆
Laurus nobilis	Bay	🪴 🪴	◆
Lavandula angustifolia	Common lavender	🪴 🪴	◆ ◆
Melissa officinalis	Lemon balm	🪴 🪴	◆ ◆

BOTANICAL NAME	COMMON NAME	PLANTS	SEED
Mentha × gracilis	Ginger mint	🪴🪴	▨
Monarda fistulosa	American wild bergamot	🪴	◆
Muscari comosum	Tassle hyacinth	🪴	◆
Oenothera biennis	Common evening primrose	🪴🪴	◆ ◆
Origanum vulgare	Oregano	🪴🪴	◆ ◆
Rosmarinus officinalis	Rosemary	🪴🪴	◆ ◆
Ruta graveolens	Common rue	🪴🪴	◆ ◆
Salvia officinalis	Common sage	🪴🪴	◆ ◆
Salvia officinalis 'Purpurascens'	Purple sage	🪴🪴	▨
Salvia sclarea	Clary	🪴	◆
Santolina chamaecyparissus	Cotton lavender	🪴🪴	◆
Saponaria officinalis	Soapwort	🪴	◆ ◆
Satureja montana	Winter savory	🪴	◆ ◆
Symphytum officinale	Common comfrey	🪴	◆ ◆
Teucrium chamaedrys	Wall germander	🪴	◆ ◆

Trees, shrubs and climbers

Actaea rubra	Red baneberry	🪴	◆
Acer rubrum	Red maple	🪴🪴	◆
Aesculus hippocastanum	Horse chestnut	🪴🪴	◆
Amelanchier ovalis	Snowy mespilus	🪴	◆
Arbutus unedo	Strawberry tree	🪴🪴	◆
Buxus sempervirens	Common box	🪴🪴	◆
Campsis radicans	Trumpet vine	🪴	◆
Cedrus libani	Cedar of Lebanon	🪴🪴	◆
Cistus monspeliensis	Montpelier rock rose	🪴	◆

Cut-leaved coneflower, Rudbeckia laciniata

BOTANICAL NAME	COMMON NAME	PLANTS	SEED
Citrus aurantiifolia	Lime	Cultivars only	◆
Citrus limon	Lemon	⬤	◆
Convolvulus cneorum	Shrubby bindweed	⬤ ⬤	▣
Cornus mas	Cornelian cherry	⬤ ⬤	◆
Coronilla valentina	Shrubby scorpion vetch	⬤	◆
Cotinus coggygria	Smoke tree	⬤ ⬤	◆
Daphne mezereum	Mezereon	⬤ ⬤	◆
Elaeagnus angustifolia	Oleaster	⬤	◆
Hypericum androsaemum	Tutsan	⬤	◆
Ilex aquifolium	Common holly	⬤ ⬤	◆
Jasminum humile	Yellow jasmine	⬤	◆
Jasminum officinale	Common jasmine	⬤ ⬤	◆
Laburnum anagyroides	Common laburnum	⬤	◆
Lathyrus latifolius	Broad-leaved everlasting pea	⬤ ⬤	◆ ◆
Lathyrus odoratus	Sweet pea	⬤	◆ ◆
Lathyrus odoratus 'Matucana'	Sweet pea 'Matucana'	⬤	◆
Lathyrus vernus	Spring bitter vetch	⬤ ⬤	◆
Lavatera olbia	Tree lavatera	⬤	◆
Liriodendron tulipifera	Tulip tree	⬤ ⬤	◆
Lonicera periclymenum	Common honeysuckle	⬤	◆
Mespilus germanica	Common medlar	⬤	◆
Morus nigra	Black mulberry	⬤ ⬤	◆
Myrtus communis	Common myrtle	⬤ ⬤	◆
Parthenocissus quinquefolia	Virginia creeper	⬤ ⬤	◆
Passiflora caerulea	Blue Passion flower	⬤ ⬤	◆ ◆

BOTANICAL NAME	COMMON NAME	PLANTS	SEED
Philadelphus coronarius	Common mock orange	🪴	◆
Phillyrea angustifolia	Mock privet	🪴	◆
Phlomis fruticosa	Jerusalem sage	🪴 🪴	◆
Prunus armeniaca	Apricot	Cultivars only	◆
Prunus persica	Peach	Cultivars only	◆
Rhus typhina	Stag's horn sumach	🪴	◆
Robinia pseudoacacia	False acacia	🪴	◆ ◆
Rosa × alba (forms)	White Rose of York	🪴	◆
Rosa × damascena (forms)	Damask rose	🪴	◆
Rosa gallica var. *officinalis*	Apothecary's rose	🪴	◆
Rosa gallica 'Versicolor'	Rosa mundi	🪴 🪴	◆
Rosa moschata	Musk rose	🪴	◆
Rosa rubiginosa	Sweet briar	🪴	◆
Rosa virginiana	Virginian rose	🪴	◆
Sorbus domestica	Service tree	🪴	◆
Syringa × persica	Persian lilac	🪴	◆
Taxus baccata	English yew	🪴 🪴	◆
Viburnum tinus	Laurustinus	🪴 🪴	◆
Vinca major	Greater periwinkle	🪴	◆
Vinca minor	Lesser periwinkle	🪴	◆

Scoring system

Unusual = Not listed for sale in the *RHS Plant Finder* or *The Seed Search*

Available = Available from up to 29 listed nurseries

Widely available = Available from over 30 listed nurseries

Further reading

Anthony, John *The Renaissance Garden in Britain*. Princes Risborough: Shire Publications, 1991

Campbell-Culver, Maggie *The Origin of Plants: The People and Plants That Have Shaped Britain's Garden History Since the Year 1000*. London: Headline, 2001

Fearnley-Whittingstall, Jane *The Garden, An English Love Affair: One Thousand Years of Gardening*. London: Weidenfeld & Nicholson, 2002

Hobhouse, Penelope *Plants in Garden History*. London: Pavilion, 2004

Jacques, David and van der Horst, Arend Jan *The Gardens of William and Mary*. London: Christopher Helm, 1988

Leith-Ross, Prudence *The John Tradescants: Gardeners to the Rose and Lily Queen*. London: Peter Owen, 1984

Pavord, Anna *The Tulip*. London: Bloomsbury, 1999

Quest-Ritson, Charles *The English Garden: A Social History*. London: Viking, 2001

Strong, Roy *The Renaissance Garden in England*. London: Thames and Hudson, 1979

Whalley, Robin and Jennings, Anne *Knot Gardens and Parterres: A History of the Knot Garden and How to Make One Today*. London: Barn Elms, 1998

The RHS Plant Finder

Published annually by the Royal Horticultural Society, the *Plant Finder* lists more than 65,000 plants available from 800 nurseries as well as contact details, maps and opening hours for all the nurseries listed. There is also an online version of the *Plant Finder* on the RHS website: www.rhs.org.uk

The Seed Search

Now in its 5th edition, *The Seed Search* lists over 40,000 seeds available from 500 seed suppliers, with details of where to find them. It also includes 9,000 vegetable cultivars. Compiled and edited by Karen Platt, and available online at: www.seedsearch.demon.co.uk

Common laburnum, Laburnum anagyroides, *was introduced from southern and eastern Europe c 1560*

Useful organisations and societies

The Museum of Garden History

The Museum of Garden History exists to enhance understanding and appreciation of the history and development of gardens and gardening in the UK, and was the world's first museum dedicated to this subject. Its attractions include a recreated 17th-century knot garden with historically authentic planting and collections of tools and gardening ephemera, as well as a well-stocked library.

www.museumgardenhistory.org

The Royal Horticultural Society

The RHS is the world's leading horticultural organisation and the UK's leading gardening charity dedicated to advancing horticulture and promoting good gardening. It offers free horticultural advice and a seed service for its members and has plant centres at its four flagship gardens.

www.rhs.org.uk

The Garden History Society

The Garden History Society aims to promote the study of the history of gardening, landscape gardens and horticulture, and to promote the protection and conservation of historic parks, gardens and designed landscapes and advise on their restoration. The Society runs a series of lectures, tours and events throughout the year.

www.gardenhistorysociety.org

The National Council for the Conservation of Plants and Gardens

The NCCPG seeks to conserve, document, promote and make available Britain and Ireland's garden plants for the benefit of horticulture, education and science. Its National Plant Collection scheme has 630 National Collections held in trust by private owners, specialist growers, arboreta, colleges, universities and botanic gardens.

www.nccpg.com

The Henry Doubleday Research Association

HDRA is a registered charity, and Europe's largest organic membership organisation. It is dedicated to researching and promoting organic gardening, farming and food. The HDRA's Heritage Seed Library saves hundreds of old and unusual vegetable varieties for posterity, also distributing them to its members. The HDRA currently manages the kitchen garden at Audley End, Essex, for English Heritage and runs Yalding Organic Gardens.

www.hdra.org.uk

Centre for Organic Seed Information

Funded by DEFRA and run by the National Institute of Agricultural Botany and the Soil Association, the Centre for Organic Seed Information is a 'one-stop shop' for sourcing certified-organic seed from listed suppliers. It covers fruits, vegetables, grasses, herbs and ornamental plants among others.

www.cosi.org.uk

Places to visit

Boscobel House
Brewood
Bishop's Wood
Shropshire ST19 9AR
Tel: 01902 850244
www.english-heritage.org.uk

Buckland Abbey
Yelverton
Devon PL20 6EY
Tel: 01822 853607
E-mail: bucklandabbey@ntrust.org.uk
www.nationaltrust.org.uk

Burton Agnes hall
Burton Agnes
Driffield
East Yorkshire YO25 0ND
Tel: 01262 490324

Haddon Hall
Bakewell
Derbyshire DE45 1LA
Tel: 01629 812855
E-mail: info@haddonhall.co.uk
www.haddonhall.co.uk

Ham House
Ham
Richmond
Surrey TW10 7RS
Tel: 020 8940 1950
E-mail: hamhouse@ntrust.org.uk
www.nationaltrust.org.uk

Hampton Court Palace
East Molesey
Surrey KT8 9AU
Tel: 0870 752 7777
www.hrp.org.uk

Hardwick Hall
Doe Lea
Chesterfield
Derbyshire S44 5QJ
Tel: 01246 850430
E-mail: hardwickhall@ntrust.org.uk
www.nationaltrust.org.uk

Hatfield House
Hatfield
Hertfordshire AL9 5NQ
Tel: 01707 287010
www.hatfield-house.co.uk

Herstmonceux Castle
Hailsham
East Sussex BN27 1RN
Tel: 01323 834457
www.herstmonceux-castle.com

Holdenby House
Holdenby
Northamptonshire NN6 8DJ
Tel: 01604 770074
E-mail: enquiries@holdenby.com
www.holdenby.com

Kenilworth Castle
Castle Green
Kenilworth
Warwickshire CV8 1NE
Tel: 01926 852 078
www.english-heritage.org.uk

Little Moreton Hall
Congleton
Cheshire CW12 4SD
Tel: 01260 272018
E-mail: littlemoretonhall@ntrust.org.uk
www.nationaltrust.org.uk

Lyveden New Bield
Nr Oundle
Peterborough
Northamptonshire PE8 5AT
Tel: 01832 205358
E-mail: lyvedennewbield@ntrust.org.uk
www.nationaltrust.org.uk

Melbourne Hall
Church Square
Melbourne
Derbyshire DE73 1EN
Tel: 01332 862502
www.melbournehall.com

Montacute House
Montacute
Somerset TA15 6XP
Tel: 01935 823289
E-mail: montacute@ntrust.org.uk
www.nationaltrust.org.uk

Moseley Old Hall
Fordhouses
Wolverhampton
Staffordshire WV10 7HY
Tel: 01902 782808
E-mail: moseleyoldhall@ntrust.org.uk
www.nationaltrust.org.uk

Tudor House Museum and Garden
Bugle Street
Southampton
Hampshire SO14 2AD
Tel: 023 8063 5904
E-mail: historic.sites@southampton.gov.uk
www.southampton.gov.uk/leisure/heritage

Acknowledgements and picture credits

English Heritage and the Museum of Garden History would like to thank the many individuals who contributed to this volume, in particular Rowan Blaik for technical editing and James O Davies for photography. Thanks to the Royal Botanic Gardens Kew for allowing access to the gardens for photography.

The author would like to acknowledge the invaluable assistance of Jane Wilson, Fiona Hope and Philip Norman at the Museum of Garden History.

Unless otherwise stated images are © English Heritage. All English Heritage photographs taken by James O Davies, except 36, 39 (Christopher Gallagher), 40, 41 (Andrew Tryner), 57 & 60 (Anne Hyde), 65 (Clay Perry), 83. Original artwork by Judith Dobie. Other illustrations reproduced by kind permission of:

AKG images: fc (Erich Lessing), 87; Ashmolean Museum, Oxford: 30, 76; Bridgeman Art Library: 6 (Ham House, Surrey, UK, The Stapleton Collection), 13 (Philip Mould, Historical Portraits Ltd, London, UK), 18 (Villa Medici, Rome, Italy), 19 (Villa Lante delle Rovere, Bagnaia, Italy), 21, 22, 61 (Private Collection, The Stapleton Collection), 23 (Villa d'Este, Tivoli, Rome, Italy), 38, 64 (© Yale Centre for British Art, Paul Mellon Collection, USA); The British Library: 2 (Cotton MS Titus D.iv, f.12v), 14 (Add 78342 57–8); Dr Chris Mullen: 52, 53; David Austin® Roses: 24; Hatfield House: 56, 58, 77; Jacques Amand: 88; Jessica Smith: 45, 68, 69, 82; The Marquess of Salisbury: 59; Museum of Garden History: 8, 10, 12, 42, 43, 44, 62, 70, 74, 75, 80; The Royal Collection © 2005, Her Majesty Queen Elizabeth II: 4; Southampton City Council Heritage Services: 26, 28, 29.

Every effort has been made to trace copyright holders and we apologise in advance for any unintentional omissions or errors, which we would be pleased to correct in any subsequent edition of the book.

About the author

Anne Jennings is a freelance garden designer, consultant and writer, and Head of Horticulture at the Museum of Garden History. She is the co-author of *Knot Gardens and Parterres*, published by Barn Elms, and writes for a variety of gardening magazines.

Other titles in this series

Roman Gardens
Medieval Gardens
Georgian Gardens
Victorian Gardens
Edwardian Gardens